HELISKIING

Diane Bailey

Rourke
Educational Media

rourkeeducationalmedia.com

Scan for Related Titles
and Teacher Resources

Before Reading:

Building Academic Vocabulary and Background Knowledge

Before reading a book, it is important to tap into what your child or students already know about the topic. This will help them develop their vocabulary, increase their reading comprehension, and make connections across the curriculum.

1. Look at the cover of the book. What will this book be about?
2. What do you already know about the topic?
3. Let's study the Table of Contents. What will you learn about in the book's chapters?
4. What would you like to learn about this topic? Do you think you might learn about it from this book? Why or why not?
5. Use a reading journal to write about your knowledge of this topic. Record what you already know about the topic and what you hope to learn about the topic.
6. Read the book.
7. In your reading journal, record what you learned about the topic and your response to the book.
8. After reading the book complete the activities below.

Content Area Vocabulary
Read the list. What do these words mean?

altitude
conquer
footage
geysers
line
mountaineers
parallel
piste
powder
province
rocker
slough
terrain
transceiver
versatile

After Reading:

Comprehension and Extension Activity

After reading the book, work on the following questions with your child or students in order to check their level of reading comprehension and content mastery.

1. Why was heliskiing created? (Summarize)
2. What obstacles do heliskiers encounter that traditional skiers would not? (Asking questions)
3. Would you take up heliskiing? Why or why not? (Text to self connection)
4. How is heliskiing different from traditional skiing? How is it similar? (Summarize)
5. What role does the helicopter pilot play in heliskiing? (Asking questions)

Extension Activity

Heliskiing is the sport that uses helicopters and skiing. It becomes much more intense and extreme than traditional skiing. Think about two sports or activities you like to do. What would it look like if you mashed them together? Create a drawing that shows what your new sport or activity would look like after you mashed them together. Provide a brief explanation about it. Share your new idea with friends and family.

TABLE OF CONTENTS

FRESH POWDER

Mitch Reeves breathed in cold, clean mountain air. He looked up at the steep cliffs in front of him. Snow covered the slope as far as he could see. It was every skier's dream: fresh **powder**! In a few minutes, a helicopter would take him to the top of that mountain. Then he would ski down it. There could be cliffs to jump over or narrow passes to get through. There could be dangerous patches of loose snow. It was up to him to figure out the route he would take. Nothing had been marked because Mitch was not at a ski lodge. He was on a remote mountain in New Zealand, heliskiing with some of the best athletes in the world. Mitch was nervous, but he could not be too scared. He had to trust himself. Mitch breathed in deeply as the helicopter came, its blades chopping loudly as it got closer and closer. It was time to **conquer** the mountain.

GETTING STARTED

Crashing through fresh powder is the dream of every heliskier.

High, far, and fast! That's what heliskiers like. They want to stretch their limits. They already know how to ski. They want to take it up a notch. Helicopters carry them to reach high mountains in remote areas. When the skiers step out of the helicopter, fresh snow stretches for miles around them. No one has skied there yet.

Heliskiers make their own trails. A **piste** is a trail that has been marked for skiers. Off-piste skiing is not marked. It takes skiers off the beaten path. Heliskiers are big-mountain skiers who find difficult slopes and tackle them with style. They may find a

mountain filled with twists and turns. There could be cliffs to jump off. There may be long, open stretches to speed down. Every mountain is different. Every time they ski, they face a new challenge.

Skiing down an unmarked trail is more challenging than a regular run.

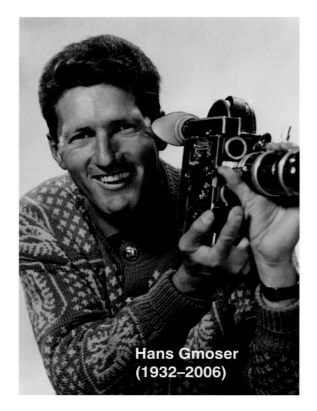

Hans Gmoser (1932–2006)

Hans Gmoser combined his movie-making skills with his love of skiing to create a new sport.

THE HISTORY OF HELISKIING

Hans Gmoser grew up in Austria. He loved the outdoors. He spent his time climbing up mountains— then skiing right back down them! Hans moved to Canada in the 1950s and began to explore the mountains there. Some of them were hard to reach. He had to climb for days just to find good places to ski.

Hans told his friend Art Patterson about this problem. Art had an idea. Why not go in a helicopter?

At first, Hans thought this was a crazy idea. Helicopters cost money, but walking was free. Still, he agreed to try it. One day in 1963, the two got in a helicopter and flew into the mountains in Western Canada. There, they found new places to ski. The trip was a success. Hans made a film about his experience. When other people saw it, they wanted to try helicopter skiing, too. Hans started a business giving heliskiing tours. A new sport was born.

Not Just Skis

Don't forget the snowboarders! Heliboarders also like to hit the high mountains. They look for new ways to challenge their snowboarding skills.

Skiing and Camping

In the early days, people who went heliskiing had to be ready for anything. One helicopter pilot took guests to remote places in Alaska. He dropped them off and they had to find their own way back. Today, there are usually lodges for people to stay in.

Heliskiing began to catch on. There were challenging mountains all over the world. People wanted to ski down all of them! The sport spread throughout the 1980s, 1990s, and 2000s. It is still growing. In the United States, people can heliski in Washington, Nevada, Colorado, and Wyoming. There are also heliski spots in New Zealand, Russia, South America, and Greenland. In the 1990s, heliskiing came to the Himalaya Mountains in Asia. They are the tallest mountains in the world. The country of Turkey is a new place where heliskiing is becoming popular.

A helicopter hovers on a Russian mountaintop to let skiers hop off.

Heliskiers carve their turns around the edge of this forest to find clean trails.

Heliskiers do not have to be experts. Intermediate skiers can try it, too. They should have a lot of practice on regular slopes and know all the basics. They should be able to turn with confidence. When they are zooming down the mountain, they need to know how to slow down and stop. They should be confident about skiing over bumps and around trees. They may need to jump off ledges and land safely on the other side. Skiers who can tackle a difficult run at a regular ski lodge may be ready to try basic heliskiing with a guide.

Two Ways to Go

Expert skiers sometimes jump out of the helicopter so that it does not have to land. Other skiers do not jump. The helicopter lands and lets them out.

SPORTS SKILLS

Heliskiers have to know a lot more than just the basics. They need to know about snow conditions and some of the challenges they will face.

The weather is always changing. So is the snow! Skiers must be prepared for a variety of conditions. Most heliskiers love powder. It is made up of small, dry particles of snow. Skiers can go fast and turn easily. It is also soft, which makes it safer in case of a fall. It can be easy to sink down into powder and go very slowly. Skiers must go fast enough to stay on top of it! After a while, fresh powder gets old. It can get wet with rain and blown

After dropping the skiers off, helicopters often stick around so that heliskiers can be filmed in action.

around by wind. It may be packed down or slippery. This type of snow is called crud and is difficult to ski on.

Sometimes a crust forms on top of the powder. It might be thick enough to support a skier's weight—or it might not. When the temperature warms up, snow melts into slush. It is wet and heavy. This is hard to ski on, too. Once the skiers leave the helicopter, they have to be ready for the snow conditions they will encounter.

Fresh powder sprays up as a heliskier powers through it. Powder can be really fun to ski in!

The view from the helicopter cockpit is breathtaking. Pilots look for new snow fields for heliskiers to conquer.

The helicopter ride to the top of the mountain is thrilling. The chopper blades pump the air as pilots fly straight up steep walls and through narrow passes. Beautiful scenery is everywhere. Skiers can enjoy the view, but they are also looking for a great place to ski.

The slope must match the skiers' ability. Experts can take on high, steep slopes. Other people will want something easier. Guides are trained to find good places. The weather may play a part. If it is snowing or windy, it may be difficult for the helicopter to fly. Fresh snow on a mountain increases the chance of an avalanche. If it is too dangerous, the guides will find a safer place.

Look Out Below!

Mountains can be dangerous places. People can fall and get trapped. Avalanches can happen. An avalanche is a huge, fast-moving flow of heavy snow. The first heliskiers were good **mountaineers**. They understood how to survive in high **altitude**.

Danger Spots

Skiers must be careful to look for sloughs. A **slough** is loose snow that can slide out from under the skier, like a mini-avalanche. They are common on snowy, untouched mountains. Heliskiers learn to avoid them.

Now that they are up on the mountain, skiers must get down. What's the best way? Nothing has been marked or mapped out. They have to find their own way down the mountain. The route they choose is called the **line**. Before they begin skiing, they study the mountain. Some skiers may want to ski through trees or over bumps and rough spots. They may want to try to get through a narrow pass. Others want the fastest, smoothest line they can get. Sometimes they have to take whatever they can find. They also make sure to look for possible danger zones. They try to plan a backup route, in case they get in trouble on the way down.

After starting from the dropoff point, a heliskier plunges through powder.

These tracks show where a pair of skiers carved parallel turns down a mountain.

Heliskiers have to get around all kinds of things on their way down a mountain. That means a lot of turning! Most intermediate and expert skiers like to do fast, smooth **parallel** turns. These let them zig-zag quickly down the mountain.

To make parallel turns, skiers put their skis about hip-width apart. Then they bend their knees in the direction of the turn. As the skis turn, they shift their weight to whichever ski is farther down the slope and then gradually shift back the other way as they go through the turn.

In the Trees

Glades are places with trees and shrubs. These are challenging for big-mountain skiers. They can also be dangerous. Trees do not bend like the guide poles on a regular ski slope. In a glade, the skier's turning skills are put to the test. The snow in glades is also unpredictable. It could be powdery or packed, depending on the weather. Skiing in glades should be done in daylight, and never alone.

This competition skier shows how experts handle bumps—knees high and ski tips up.

Buried trees, logs, and rocks can cause bumps on the mountain. Skiers must pay attention and see them coming, and then be ready to take them on. The bumps don't move, but a skier's legs do. They learn to use their legs as shock absorbers. They also make the bumps work for them. At the very top of a bump, only the middle of the ski is touching the snow. The tip and tail are free. This is a great place to turn in another direction.

Get ready to jump! Ledges and cliffs are other challenges. Some types of jumps give more air time than others, but they require more practice. Skiers tuck their legs underneath them while in the air. That stops the wind from slowing them down. They straighten their legs out before landing, but keep them slightly bent to absorb the impact.

A skier gets air off a jump, tucking in his legs to soar more easily.

GEAR UP

Heliskiers find great places to ski. They have the skills to make it down the mountain. Now they need the gear to do it safely.

Heliskiers often choose wider skis because they have more surface areas that touch the snow. This is good for powder skiing. Wider skis better distribute body weight, which helps a skier float on top of the snow.

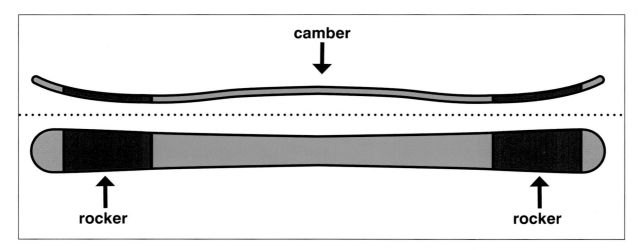

This diagram shows two views of the rocker ski—from the side and its hourglass shape from above.

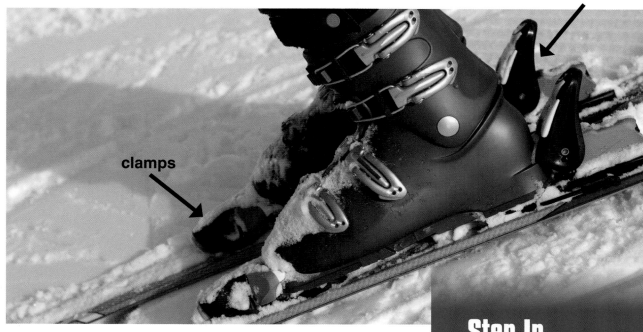

black release bars

clamps

In 2002, skier Shane McConkey designed a type of ski called a **rocker**. In a regular ski, the middle of the ski rises slightly off the ground. In a rocker, the middle rests on the ground, while the two ends curve upward. That helps skiers feel like they are floating. Rockers are also good for landing from a jump. The edges are less likely to dig into the snow and cause the skier to fall.

Step In

Ski boots connect directly to the skis with clamps at the toe and heel. The clips at the ankle form a tight fit for the skier. The support of these boots helps the skier stay in control while turning and stopping. Hitting the black bars releases the boots from the skis.

These snowboarders have to walk back up the hill to reach a new place to slide down.

Just like skis, off-piste snowboards are designed to be stable. They are often longer than regular snowboards. This helps boarders keep their balance when they are going fast or landing from a jump. Some also come in a rocker shape. That helps riders stay on the surface of the snow. These snowboards usually have a wide nose that skims over the top of the snow. A deep notch in the tail makes turning easier.

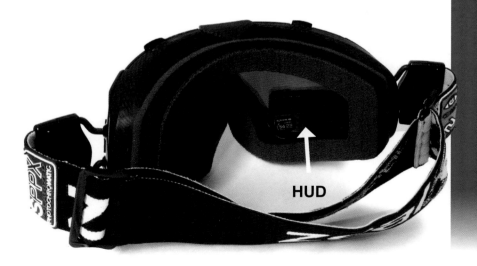

HUD

Heads Up!

Skiers wear goggles to cut the glare of sunlight bouncing off the snow. Goggles also protect the eyes from blowing snow. Some fancier goggles do even more. They come with an electronic heads-up display (HUD). The HUD displays information on the inside of the goggles. It shows data about speed, altitude, and location. It can keep track of how many runs a skier took and how long a jump lasted. Heliskiing has gone high tech!

All of a sudden, the snow begins to loosen and shift. Crack! A loud noise thunders over the mountain. Tons of snow begins sliding down. Avalanche! This is a dangerous risk for big-mountain skiers.

Heliskiers carry basic avalanche safety gear. A shovel helps them dig. Some bring a long, folding pole called

This pair of skiers is exploring the edge of where an avalanche just stopped.

a probe. It lets skiers poke the snow to search for people who have been buried. A **transceiver** sends out electronic signals that will help rescuers find people trapped in the snow.

Sometimes skiers wear airbags. They will inflate in

Dogs trained to sniff out people under the snow can help locate avalanche victims.

an avalanche. They allow skiers to float on the surface of the snow. Some skiers carry a special breathing machine. It can suck air from the skier's clothing and from the surrounding snow. That can keep a skier alive until rescuers arrive.

An airplane cannot land in a tiny spot on the top of a mountain. That's why heliskiers need helicopters. Helicopters are more **versatile** than planes. Helicopters can go straight up and down. That lets them take off and land in small, cramped spots. They can also turn in tight circles,

No airplane could land on this mountain peak, but a helicopter has room to stop and drop off skiers.

and hover in one place. This makes them ideal for getting to hard-to-reach places.

Heliskiers go to high altitudes. The tops of some mountains might be 15,000 feet (4,572 meters) high or more. The air is thinner at those altitudes. It is more difficult to control a helicopter in thin air. Special helicopters are designed to fly in such air. They have extra climbing power through the thin atmosphere. They can also fly well even when there is wind and snow. Heliskiing helicopters are roomy enough to carry several passengers with all their gear. They also fly fast, so there is more time left for skiing!

After leaving the skiers on the mountain, the helicopter returns to its base.

THE STARS

Expert skiers can rip down a mountain at 70 miles (112 kilometers) per hour. They shred the snow, doing daredevil turns and jumps. They flip in mid-air—and nail the landings! At the same time they have to look out for dangerous obstacles. Heliskiing is the perfect way to tackle all those challenges. Take a look at some of the top stars of the slopes!

The baskets on the side of the chopper hold the skiers' gear until they reach the dropoff point.

SETH MORRISON

Seth Morrison has been skiing for more than 20 years. Seth grew up in Colorado and decided in high school to focus on a career in skiing. It was a good decision. He has won several ski events and

Seth Morrison shows perfect form as he carves through fresh powder.

appeared in more than 30 movies. He has had some trouble along the way. He was in a helicopter crash and once was buried in an avalanche. Luckily, he made it out! Soon he was back on the slopes, looking for the next good run.

INGRID BACKSTROM

On a steep slope, Ingrid Backstrom has to slide between trees and bushes.

Ingrid Backstrom is one of the best-known women in the sport. She is from Normandy Park, Washington, and grew up skiing. Her family hit the slopes almost every weekend. Now, Ingrid makes her living as a skier. She has been in several movies about extreme skiing. They have taken her to remote places in the Arctic, Antarctica, and Alaska. That means spending a lot of time in a helicopter. She even married a helicopter pilot!

ESSEX PRESCOTT

Essex Prescott is from Idaho and went to college in British Columbia, Canada. He moved there to be close to good mountains for skiing. In 2014 Essex competed at the World Heli Challenge, a competition for heliskiers. His team did not win, but they never gave up. Essex was the one leading and cheering them on all the way. The Shane McConkey Award is named for a popular skier who died in 2009. Essex won this award because of his love for the sport.

Can you spot Essex Prescott at the bottom of the newly carved ski trail?

HOT SPOTS FOR COLD SPORTS

Expert heliskiers travel the world looking for the best slopes. They know where to find different kinds of **terrain**. Some skiers like ramps for jumping. Some look for steep walls. Others want narrow spines, like the peak of a roof. Skiers have to stay right on top of these ridges, sometimes only a pair of skis wide.

Heliskiing began in the **province** of British Columbia in Western Canada. It still has the most places to heliski. British Columbia is good for large, open bowls of snow. For more adventure, heliskiers can go to Alaska. It has very high, steep peaks. Russia is a great place for scenery. Skiers can see glaciers and **geysers**. Skiers might zoom past bears on their way down. They can even ski into the crater of a volcano.

Huge bowls of fresh powder make British Columbia a heliskiing hot spot.

MAKING MOVIES

Some of the best skiers in the world are not just athletes. They are also movie stars! They appear in films that show off their best moves. Some cameramen film the action from the ground. Others ride in the helicopter to shoot from above. Helicopter pilots are specially trained to fly so that the cameramen can get good shots.

Often things do not go right the first time. Skiers must try runs and jumps several times before they get the perfect

shot. After all the filming is finished, the **footage** is put together into a movie. Amateur heliskiers can make movies, too. There are

Helicopters used in filming carefully hover over the skiers as they make their moves.

special cameras designed to be mounted on skiers' bodies or helmets. That way they do not have to carry them.

Ski Movie Tips

Ski movies work best when they show the action from different angles. What does it look like from above? What is the scene from below? How about the skier's point of view? Also, people in ski movies often use bright colored boards to show up well against the snow.

WORLD HELI CHALLENGE

The World Heli Challenge is a contest that started in 1995. It is held in Wanaka, New Zealand. It attracts some of the best heliskiers and heliboarders in the world. Contestants try to earn a place in the event by making a video and posting it online. The organizers of the World Heli Challenge watch all the videos to find the best athletes. People can also vote for their favorite teams.

Only two teams make it through to the final competition. It is a two-day, head-to-head shootout. Each team has two athletes, plus a cameraman who films all the action. At the end, they put a film together. Judges choose the final winners. They look at the athletes' technical skill and the quality of the movie.

No slope? No problem for skiers taking part in the World Heli Challenge. 41

DOWN THE MOUNTAIN

As he stood at the top of the mountain, Mitch Reeves felt like he was in another world. It was a totally different zone. The cliffs were bigger. The risk was bigger. It was like everything had been multiplied by ten! There was only one way to the top—in a helicopter. And, there was only one way down—on his skis.

Heliskiers travel a thin line between danger and excitement.

Mitch liked to go fast. He liked to jump off cliffs. He was getting good at turns and flips. Now, he wanted to put all those skills to the test. Mitch saw a cliff at the bottom of the run that he wanted to jump off. Things had to go perfectly. There had to be good snow. He had to get just the right position. It was a difficult move, but it would be awesome if he pulled it off. It would look good on film, too! Could he do it?

Mitch Reeves gathers speed as he heads down toward a jump.

Mitch Reeves flies over the jump, soaring like a bird before sticking the landing!

Mitch knew he was taking a chance. He felt as if his big chance was right in front of him. He was a strong skier and he had good equipment. He trusted his skills. Skiing at this level meant he had to be prepared physically and mentally. Mitch felt like he was ready. He was confident he could do it.

As the helicopter flew away, he started down the mountain. The cliff got closer and closer. There was no turning back now. He zoomed off the cliff, soared through the air, and then—yes!—he landed it! That was one exciting jump! Mitch had made it. Now, he could start thinking about the next move, which was just seconds away. For heliskiers, that's what it's all about: finding the next move and the best way down the mountain.

Heliskiing adventure means an open field, a daring skier, and someone high above to get them there—then take pictures!

GLOSSARY

altitude (AL-tih-tood): the height or distance above the ground

conquer (KAHNG-ker): take control of

footage (FOOT-ij): all the film that is taken for a movie, before it has been put together into the final cut

geysers (GUY-zers): places where hot water and steam shoot out of the ground

line (LINE): the route a skier chooses to ski down a mountain

mountaineers (mown-ti-NEERS): people who climb mountains

parallel (PARE-uh-lell): describing two objects that are next to each other and have the same distance between them

piste (PEEST): a marked trail that is prepared for skiers

powder (POW-der): a type of snow made up of small, dry particles

province (PRAH-vince): a state or territory in Canada

rocker (ROK-er): a type of ski that has a slight U-shape, with the ends higher than the middle

slough (SLOO): loose snow that can slide, like a small avalanche

terrain (tuh-RANE): the type of land in an area, such as hilly or flat

transceiver (tran-SEE-ver): a device that sends out electronic signals for tracking

versatile (VER-suh-tuhl): able to do many different things

INDEX

SHOW WHAT YOU KNOW

1. What are three popular places for heliskiing?

2. Why are heliskis longer than regular skis?

3. What is glade skiing?

4. What safety gear can heliskiers carry?

5. How do teams enter the World Heli Challenge?

WEBSITES TO VISIT:

www.worldhelichallenge.com

www.adventure.howstuffworks.com/outdoor-activities/snow-sports/heli-skiing.htm

www.purepowder.com/heliskiing/whatisheliskiing.cfm

ABOUT THE AUTHOR

Diane Bailey has written about 40 nonfiction books for kids and teens, on topics ranging from science to sports to celebrities. Diane also works as a freelance editor, helping authors who write novels for children and young adults. Diane has two sons, two dogs, and lives in Kansas.

Meet The Author!
www.meetREMauthors.com

www.rourkeeducationalmedia.com

PHOTO CREDITS: Cover © TKTKTKT
Interior: Image Source: 1; CMH Heli-Skiing: 8; Dreamstime.com (© photographers): Genna Poltaratska 4; photographerlondon 6; Merkushev 7; Neilneil 9; Lexan 11; Steve Rosset 12, 19, 21, 37; Roberto Caucino 13, 31; Daizuokin 15; Soren Egeberg 16, 30; Kapu 17; Monkey Business Images 18; Annemario 20; Chudakov 23; Gary Blakeley 24; Rawpixelimages 27; Peter Lovas 28; David Schliepp 29; Ilsa Maski 32; Francesca Perticucci 38; RubySunday 42. Recon Instruments: 26. Shutterstock: GTS Productions 22; Mountainpix 39. Skiers Edge Pro: 25.
© Tony Harrington: 33, 34, 35, 41, 43, 45.
Background image: Dreamstime.com/Genna Poltaratska.

Edited by: Keli Sipperley
Produced by Shoreline Publishing Group
Design by: Bill Madrid, Madrid Design

Library of Congress PCN Data

Heliskiing / Diane Bailey
(Intense Sports)
ISBN 978-1-63430-441-2 (hard cover)
ISBN 978-1-63430-541-9 (soft cover)
ISBN 978-1-63430-629-4 (e-Book)
Library of Congress Control Number: 2015932636

Also Available as:
ROURKE'S
e-Books